NEW BEGINNINGS IN CHRIST

DR. DARRELL HUFFMAN

26 25 24 23 22   8 7 6 5 4 3 2 1

New Beginnings
Copyright ©2023 Darrell Huffman

Scripture taken from the New King James Version®. Copyright © 1982 by Thomas Nelson. Used by permission. All rights reserved.

All Rights Reserved. Except as permitted under the U.S. Copyright Act of 1976, no part of this publication may be reproduced, distributed, or transmitted in any form by any means, or stored in a database or retrieval system, without the prior written permission of the author and/or publisher.

Published by:
Emerge Publishing, LLC
9521 B Riverside parkway, Suite 243
Tulsa, OK 74137
Phone: 888.407.4447
www.emerge.pub

Library of Congress Cataloging-in-Publication Data:
ISBN: 978-1954966-22-2 Perfect Bound

Printed in the United States

Contents

Chapter 1 Beginning Your New Life 1

Chapter 2 Make Sure Proof
of Your Salvation 8

Chapter 3 Following Jesus in Baptism 35

Chapter 4 Being Filled with
the Holy Spirit 62

Chapter 1

Beginning Your New Life

"For God so loved the world that He gave His only begotten Son, that whoever believes in Him should not perish but have everlasting life. For God did not send His Son into the world to condemn the world, but that the world through Him might be saved" (John 3:16-17 NKJV).

Because of God's great love for us, He sent His Son Jesus to bring full redemption to all. Jesus did not come to bring us into religion. He did not come to condemn us for our sin and rebellion against God. Jesus came for one reason, to bring us out of our sin that separated us from God into a salvation that would not only forgive our sins, but would totally change our nature from sin to righteousness.

Jesus came to bring us back into spiritual life and to reunite us with our Heavenly Father. Colossians 1:12-19 says, "Giving thanks to the Father, Who has qualified *and* made us fit to share the portion which is the inheritance of the saints (God's holy people) in the Light. [The Father] has delivered *and* drawn us to Himself out of the control *and* the dominion of darkness and has transferred us into the kingdom of the Son of His love, In Whom we have our redemption *through His blood*, [which means] the forgiveness of our sins. [Now] He is the exact likeness of the unseen God [the visible representation of the invisible]; He is the Firstborn of all creation. For it was in Him that all things were created, in heaven and on earth, things seen and things unseen, whether thrones, dominions, rulers, or authorities; all things were created *and* exist through Him [by His service, intervention] and in *and* for Him. And He Himself existed before all things, and in Him all things consist (cohere, are held together). He also is the Head of [His] body, the church; seeing He is the Beginning, the Firstborn from among the dead, so that He alone in everything *and* in every respect might occupy the chief place [stand first and be preeminent].

For it has pleased [the Father] that all the divine fullness (the sum total of the divine perfection, powers, and attributes) should dwell in Him permanently." (AMPC).

When we accept Jesus as our Lord and Savior, we are told in verse 14 that we have full redemption and our sins are forgiven and remitted through His blood. We are cleansed from our past and from all our wrong actions and deeds. Our sin and sin nature are washed away by the offering of the blood of Jesus. In verse 13, we see a truth that is so great that it is sometimes hard to grasp with our minds.

We see the reason that Jesus died, was buried and arose from the dead. We see the reason of His redemptive work. That reason was so God could deliver us from the power and authority of satan and sin and then draw us to Himself and make us His own sons and daughters. Through the redemptive work of Jesus, we are now delivered out of the kingdom of darkness and brought into the Kingdom of God.

The devil no longer has any authority over the born-again child of God. We are no longer under the influence or control of the kingdom of darkness and sin. Jesus is now our Lord and we are now citizens of the Kingdom of God. With this new life we are now brought into a righteous relationship with God that places us in a position to partake of God's Inheritance of blessing and provision. We now look to God as our source and we put our lives and eternity in His Hands.

II Corinthians 5:14-17 says, "For the love of Christ compels us, because we judge thus: that if One died for all, then all died; and He died for all, that those who live should live no longer for themselves, but for Him who died for them and rose again.

Therefore, from now on, we regard no one according to the flesh. Even though we have known Christ according to the flesh, yet now we know *Him thus* no longer. Therefore, if anyone *is* in Christ, *he is* a new creation; old things have passed away; behold, all things have become new." (NKJV). Here again we see that when we make Jesus our Lord, God makes us to become new creations in Christ. The moment you accept Jesus in your heart, God puts your past away, takes out your sin nature and puts a new heart filled with His nature in you. You become a brand-new person in Christ with no past filled with sin and rebellion for all is wiped clean by the blood of Jesus.

Now let's take a moment and look back at verses 14-15, "For the love of Christ compels us, because we judge thus: that if One died for all, then all died;

and He died for all, that those who live should live no longer for themselves, but for Him who died for them and rose again." (NKJV). Notice that Paul says that when Christ died, we all died with Him. When Jesus was on the cross bearing our sin and shame, we were there with Him. Jesus was our representative. He was there in our behalf. When Jesus was raised up from the dead, we were raised up with Him.

Ephesians 2:4-6 says, "But God, who is rich in mercy, because of His great love with which He loved us, even when we were dead in trespasses, made us alive together with Christ (by grace you have been saved), and raised *us* up together, and made *us* sit together in the heavenly *places* in Christ Jesus" (NKJV). When we accept Jesus as our Lord, God raises us up to the place He created for us in Christ. Now old things have passed away and all things become new. But notice again in verse 15 that Paul says that when we make Jesus our Lord, we are making the decision and commitment to now live in this new life in Christ.

Christianity is not a one-time decision to accept Jesus at an altar. Christianity is a decision and commitment to give our heart and life to God and to begin to live this new life He has given us in Christ Jesus. Christianity is a new beginning with a new life that is now given to us by God's grace through faith in Jesus Christ.

In Acts 2 after the Holy Spirit has been poured out on the 120 in the upper room, the apostle Peter preaches a powerful message on the life, death, burial and resurrection of the Lord Jesus. In verses 36-39, we read, ""Therefore let all the house of Israel know assuredly that God has made this Jesus, whom you crucified, both Lord and Christ." Now when they heard *this*, they were cut to the heart, and said to Peter and the rest of the apostles, "Men *and* brethren, what shall we do?" Then Peter said to them, "Repent, and let every one of you be baptized in the name of Jesus Christ for the remission of sins; and you shall receive the gift of the Holy Spirit. For the promise is to you and to your children, and to all who are afar off, as many as the Lord our God will call." (NKJV).

After hearing this powerful message of God's love, the people asked Peter to show them how to receive this great salvation and how to begin this new life in Christ. In verse 38, Peter give them three steps to begin their new life in and with Christ.

First, he tells them to repent, to change their views and ways and turn to the Lord with all their heart.

True repentance is to turn your heart, life, lifestyle and eternity over to Jesus. It is an act of surrender, of realizing you can't save yourself and turning to the Lord Jesus to bring salvation into your heart and life.

Second, he tells them to be baptized. Water baptism is a witness to the world that we have given our lives to Jesus and we are no longer our own. We in baptism declare that we died with Christ, we were buried with Christ, and we have been raised up into our new life in Christ.

Third, he tells them to receive the gift of the Holy Spirit. Once we are born of the Spirit, we need to receive the gift and infilling of the Holy Spirit. In Acts 1:8, the Lord Jesus gives us the purpose of receiving the gift of the Holy Spirit. He says, "But you shall receive power when the Holy Spirit has come upon you; and you shall be witnesses to Me in Jerusalem, and in all Judea and Samaria, and to the end of the earth." (NKJV).

In the next three Chapters we will look at each of these three steps in helping us to begin to live the new life in Jesus. It is so important that we follow God's Word and not the opinions of man or religion. May we all build our lives on the solid rock of our Lord Jesus Christ and His Word.

Chapter 2

Make Sure Proof of Your Salvation

"Let this mind be in you which was also in Christ Jesus, who, being in the form of God, did not consider it robbery to be equal with God, but made Himself of no reputation, taking the form of a bondservant, *and* coming in the likeness of men. And being found in appearance as a man, He humbled Himself and became obedient to *the point of* death, even the death of the cross. Therefore God also has highly exalted Him and given Him the name which is above every name, that at the name of Jesus every knee should bow, of those in heaven, and of those on earth, and of those under the earth, and *that* every tongue should confess that Jesus Christ *is* Lord, to the glory of God the Father. Therefore, my beloved, as you have always obeyed, not as in my presence only, but now much more in my absence, work out your own salvation with fear and trembling for it is God who works within you both to will and to do for His good pleasure" (Philippians 2:5-13 NKJV).

In this second chapter of Philippians, the apostle Paul is speaking to the children of God. He's speaking to the church, and he's telling them to fulfill his joy and live for God. Then he talks about letting Jesus's mind be in you. You begin to see yourself the way God sees you. You begin to understand what God did for you through Jesus Christ, how Jesus died, the death on the cross. He took your place, and He took your sin. Then God raised Him up and gave Him a name above every name. And at the name of Jesus, every knee must bow: things in heaven, things in earth, and things beneath the earth. He also says that every tongue must confess Jesus is Lord (see verses 9-10).

In verse 12, Paul says, "Therefore, my beloved, as you have always obeyed, not as in my presence only, but now much more in my absence, work out your own salvation with fear and trembling for it is God who works within you both to will and to do for His good pleasure." What I wanted to touch on here is this "work out your own salvation with fear and trembling." What does that mean? Can you save yourself? Absolutely not.

But what he is telling them is this: You take responsibility for your own salvation. Don't trust your eternal life to somebody else. Don't trust your eternal life to a preacher, a church, a denomination, or a religious faction.

Do not trust your eternal life to somebody else's opinion or what somebody else might think. He's saying, "You make sure you take care of your own salvation."

When we all die and stand before the Lord Jesus Christ, I'll not give an account for your life. I'll give an account for my life. Whenever I stand before the Lord, it will not be me standing there saying, "Well, you know, Lord, I trusted So-and-so, and our church didn't preach it that way. Our church didn't believe it just like that. After all, I heard this minister say—" God will say, "That has nothing to do with what you did about my Son. What did you do about the commandments that I gave you from my holy written Word? Did you not read that? I said that Jesus died for your sins and that you were to put on His mind and that you were to work out your own salvation." Paul said that it is God that desires to work in your life, both to will and to do it for His good pleasure. Don't you see that it is not what man thinks, what the church thinks, or what religion thinks, but it is what God has said to you that counts? It is God's will in your life. That is most important.

Notice Paul said that you followed the commandments, honored the commandments and obeyed the commandments not only when people were looking at you, but when you were by yourself. Anybody can act saved in church. When the preachers had gone out to lunch with them or when the deacons are standing around, anybody can act saved.

But how do you act when nobody's around? True salvation is not just to put on a front. In verse 3, he said, "Let nothing be done through selfish ambition or conceit, but in lowliness of mind let each esteem others better than himself" (Philippians 2:3 NKJV). Some translations use "strife and vainglory." He's saying, you're just doing it out of your vanity to get glory, to let everybody see how spiritual you are. Or "I go to church and that's okay."

It is important to us each one, individually, to make sure that we have worked out our own salvation. I want to know that I know that I'm born again. I want to know that I'm ready for God. I want to know that God is working in me both to will and to do for His good pleasure.

I want to know that I'm saved when I'm in my lowliest hour. I want to know that I'm saved when there's nobody around. I want to know that I'm saved when it's the darkest hour of my life. I want to know that I'm saved at the midnight hour of my life and in the crisis that I'm facing. I want to know that if this is my last breath, I can take it with confidence that the next sight I'll see will be gloryland. I'll be caught up into eternity with the Lord Jesus Christ. Paul says, "Work it out; do something about it."

So many people in hell right now had good intentions in all their life. They were going to do something about getting saved. "I'm going to do this someday. I'm going to have to get saved."

I talked to a gentleman not too long ago, and he said, "Yeah, yeah, I'm getting older. I'm going to need to come to church and do something about that." This man was aware of his need of salvation. He knew if he were to die, he'd go to hell, but he's not doing anything about it. Too many people are letting sin live in their lives. They're letting the world dictate to them what they're doing. They're letting religion tell them, "After all, if you go to church, you got your name on the roster. You've been in so many Sunday school classes, you're saved. You're a good person. You're a good, moral person."

But morality and being a good person and being a church attender has nothing to do with getting you saved. Not cussing is not getting you saved. We think, "I changed my life. I quit drinking. I'm a reformed alcoholic." I don't care how reformed you are. If you aren't born again, you're not saved.

You might ask, "How do you know?" Let's see how we work out our salvation. Look in Ephesians 2:1-10 to get a better picture of what I'm talking about with working out your salvation by accepting Jesus Christ and making sure of your relationship with God.

"And you hath he quickened, who were dead in trespasses and sins; Wherein in time past ye walked according to the course of this world, according to the prince of the power of the air, the spirit that now worketh in the children of disobedience: Among whom also we all had our conversation in times past in the lusts of our flesh, fulfilling the desires of the flesh and of the mind; and were by nature the children of wrath, even as others. But God, who is rich in mercy, for his great love wherewith he loved us, Even when we were dead in sins, hath quickened us together with Christ, (by grace ye are saved;) And hath raised us up together, and made us sit together in heavenly places in Christ Jesus: That in the ages to come he might shew the exceeding riches of his grace in his kindness toward us through Christ Jesus. For by grace are ye saved through faith; and that not of yourselves: it is the gift of God: Not of works, lest any man should boast. For we are his workmanship, created in Christ Jesus unto good works, which God hath before ordained that we should walk in them." (KJV).

"You hath He quickened" he's talking to you that were dead in trespasses and that means it was added at the translator's discretion trying to show you that the intent of this chapter is to show you that God has saved you and what He saved you out of.

Verse 2 says you walked under the nature of this world. There was a spirit of disobedience that operated in you, and then he says we were fulfilling our flesh and mind's desires. If just of the flesh was enough, just of the mind, you could go reeducate yourself. You could go to college, educate your mind, get your PhD in philosophy, and you'd be alright, and you could quit drinking, quit smoking, eat the right foods, and you'd be okay. But it's just not the lust of the flesh, and it's just not the problem with the mind. He says in the final part of verse 3 that it's not only your mind that causes you to sin in your flesh, but you had the wrong nature. The

Bible says in Romans 3:23, "For all have sinned and come short of the glory of God" (KJV). Romans 3:10 says, "There is none righteous, no, not one" (KJV). The Bible also tells us in Romans 5:12 that because of Adam's sin, spiritual death, separation from God, and the nature of Satan has passed on all men and all people. Therefore, we have a nature problem. You have a heart problem. So he says you were by nature, the children of wrath; you operated under the power of darkness, under the spirit of disobedience, under the god of this world: Satan. He ruled your life.

Now look what he says in Ephesians 2:4-7: "But God, who is rich in mercy, for his great love wherewith he loved us, Even when we were dead in sins, hath quickened us together with Christ, (by grace ye are saved;) And hath raised us up together, and made us sit together in heavenly places in Christ Jesus: That in the ages to come he might shew the exceeding riches of his grace in his kindness toward us through Christ Jesus. (KJV) He's saying, "Yeah, you might be able to do something with your head." Most religions take care of your mind until you get in a pickle. Then you revert back to your nature, and you beat your wife, kick your kids, gun down your neighbor, and everything else. You say, "I don't know what came over me." I'll tell you what came over you. There was that nature that you couldn't educate out of you. You're doing really good until you get under a crisis. Then you reach for the cigarette, for the dope, for the beer, for this, for that, or the sex because you can keep your flesh under control in normal circumstances. But when it isn't normal, your flesh will rise back up. Why? "Because something came over me and I couldn't control my flesh anymore." It was the nature.

God looked down, and He said, "Listen, they can't do it. So here's what I'm going to do. I'm going to send my Son and He's going to come in the form of a servant. He's going to take on their sin and die the death on the cross. And He's going to take their punishment. When I raise Him up and make His name Lord, I'm going to raise them up with Him and quicken and make them alive together with Him. I'm going to save them, and I'm going to pour my grace into them. The works that they've got to do is to release faith in the finished work of Jesus Christ. When they release faith in my Son, I'll come into them and take the old nature out and put in a new nature; take the old heart out, put a new heart in; and I'll raise them up. They'll be the workmanship of my hand." God says, "I'll recreate you and make you a brand-new creation that never existed before. I'll make you a brand-new species of being that never lived before. I'll make you my sons and daughters."

What is the work of our salvation faith in the grace of Almighty God? It is accepting what Jesus has done for us. It is not trying to get good on my own. It is not trying to reeducate my life. It is not trying to reform myself. It is not trying to cope with the stress and the problems of life, but it is accepting Jesus Christ as my Lord and my Savior and allowing God to work both His will and His purpose and His plan in my life.

We become God's workmanship. That's why I can stand up and say, "I'm a new creature in Christ Jesus. Old things are passed away. All things have become new. I'm not a reformed alcoholic. I'm a new creation. Praise God. I'm not a reformed drug addict. I'm a new creation in Christ Jesus. I'm not an old sinner saved by grace. I was an old sinner. Now I'm the workmanship of God, and He has ordained me to walk in His blessings."

How do I release my faith? Let's look at Romans 10:8. We're talking about the word of faith. We're talking about grace. We're talking about making sure of your own salvation, making sure that you're ready to meet the master, making sure that you are born again.

Jesus told Nicodemus in John 3 that you must be born again. In Luke 13:3, He said, "Except ye repent, ye shall all likewise perish" (KJV). Peter said it is not God's will that any should perish, but that all should come to repentance (see 2 Peter 3:9). We need a change of life, a change of lordship, a change of direction, a change in the way we believe and what we do concerning God. In Matthew 18:3, Jesus said, "Verily I say unto you, Except ye be converted, and become as little children, ye shall not enter into the kingdom of heaven." (KJV). We must become a child of God.

Romans 10:8 says, "But what saith it? 'The Word is nigh thee, even in thy mouth, and in thy heart: that is, the word of faith, which we preach" (KJV). What is that word of faith? Since it's faith and grace that get you saved. We have to work in faith because he said in Ephesians 2:8 that by grace, you're saved through faith. Paul told the Philippians to work out their own salvation. The only way I can work it out is through faith.

So what is that? Romans 10:9 says, "That if thou shalt confess with thy mouth the Lord Jesus, and shalt believe in thine heart that God hath raised Him from the dead, thou shalt be saved" (KJV). He's saying that if I believe that Jesus Christ is the son of God and He came to this Earth for my sake, like John 3:16 says; I believe that He died for my sins; I believe that God raised Him from the dead and I accept that; and then I confess Him as my Lord, I'll be saved. Romans 10:10 says, "For with the heart man believeth unto righteousness; and with the mouth confession is made unto salvation" (KJV). That's how easy it is to be born again. That is the spiritual formula for the work that it takes to bring salvation into your life. Once you've done that, the Bible says you're born again.

Somebody says, "Oh, I can do that." There's no catch. I just want you to see the fullness of what you're doing when you accept Jesus as Lord. I want you to see the fullness of what you're committing to. When you believe on the Lord Jesus Christ and confess Him as Lord with your mouth, I want you to see that the Bible says now that you are required to work out your salvation. You can't do it by works, but faith must have corresponding actions or it's dead. I can't just say this. I've got to commit to it and say, "It's right."

When he says in verse 10 that with the heart, man believes it, he's saying the heart of man reaches out, grabs a hold of it, and retains it, won't let go of it.

What is God requiring of me to come to Him and receive salvation? He said I had to do it by faith. I've got to receive His grace by faith. And James said faith without works is dead faith (see James 2:20). Without corresponding actions, faith without follow-up is dead. So what is God requiring of me? Look in Titus 2 for some instruction on this new birth. We're not talking about works, trying to get in on our own merit. We're talking about releasing our faith and making a commitment to God. Everybody wants to live for God as long as it doesn't cost them anything. Everybody wants to live for God as long as it doesn't interfere in their lifestyle. Everybody wants to live for God as long as they can get to heaven and not do anything else on the way.

"For the grace of God that bringeth salvation hath appeared to all men, teaching us that, denying ungodliness and worldly lusts, we should live soberly, righteously, and godly, in this present world" (Titus 2:11-12 KJV). There it is again: the grace of God brings the salvation. Once again, you're saved by grace through faith. It's God's grace, His unmerited favor, God's goodness. It's God's work on Calvary that brings salvation. That grace has appeared to all men for salvation. The other thing grace does when it brings salvation to you is to teach you that grace is the nature of God.

Grace is God's nature. God's grace and God's nature comes to you and says, "My Son died for you. He gave His life on Calvary. He bore your sins. He was made to be a sin offering for you so that you could be made the righteousness of God in Him. And if you'll release faith and reach out with your faith and believe on Him and accept Him as your Lord, confess Him as your Lord, you shall be saved. I'll impart unto you eternal life." Grace comes to you and says, "I want you to live for me and serve me. I'll be your God, and you'll be my child," and it also teaches us to deny ungodliness and lust.

We've got something to do here. Salvation isn't just come to the altar, confess Jesus as Lord, and go out and live like the devil. The reason you came to the altar was so you'd quit living like the devil. Salvation means a change of sides, a change of action, a change of purpose, a change of destiny, a change of direction, a change of attitude. It means everything in you has changed. You've given up the old life so you can put on the new. God says, "If you want to come in and receive my grace and salvation, fine. But the same grace that saves you also says you've got to live for me if you're going to get it."

Jesus said, "And why call ye Me, 'Lord, Lord,' and do not the things which I say?" (Luke 6:46 KJV).

He said only those who do the will of the Father are going to enter into the kingdom of God (see Matthew 7:21).

God came to save us as a means to get us involved in His Kingdom. It means to give God your life: you're no longer your own. You belong to Him. Jesus is now Lord of your life. You're bought with a price, and you're to glorify God in your spirit and in your bodies. I know you're going to be a baby when you get born again. I know you're going to trip up on some things, but God's Word teaches you that, "Now, if you are going live for me, you're going to have to start denying those things. You're going to have to start standing against those things. You're going to have to stop letting them dominate your life. You can't go out here and live in sin anymore."

We've heard all kinds of things. People say, "Oh, if we get married, we'll lose our checks." You better get married or you are going to lose your salvation. "Well, we are going to live together for a while. See if we can make it." You better get married or you aren't going to ever make it. "I've got my career to pursue." You better pursue the person of God, you better pursue the will of God, and you better begin to pursue the glory of God and the things of God because eternity is one heartbeat away. It's not just when Jesus comes back. You could die in the next few minutes, the next breath. It doesn't matter what degree you got in your life. It doesn't matter what you've got planned. You could take your last breath and fall out of that chair and your time of decision is over. You better be ready to step over into heaven and give a good account of yourself before Almighty God. I don't care how many businesses you owned. I don't care how many jobs you gave out. I don't care how much money you made. I don't care how big your house is. I don't care how humble you've tried to be. I don't care if you lived in a log cabin just so you can stay humble all your life. That doesn't mean that you pursued the plans and purposes of God in your life.

Titus 2 goes on to say, "Teaching us that, denying ungodliness and worldly lusts, we should live soberly, righteously, and godly in this present world; looking for that blessed hope and the glorious appearing of the great God and our Savior Jesus Christ" (vv 12-13 KJV). Are you looking for Jesus? Do you get thrilled when people preach Jesus is coming back and the rapture is going to take place? Most of the church isn't excited about the possibility of Jesus coming back because they have their own agendas, their own life, their own purpose. They haven't had this done or that done. We need to get saved, live for

God, and let God be God of our life. We need to be real in this thing. You need to be able to be picked out of a lineup for being a Christian or singled out in a room because you're a Christian.

There's a different atmosphere about you, a different attitude about you, a different look about you. People look at you for a while. They finally say, "You're a Christian, aren't you?" The apostle Peter had to finally cuss and act like a sinner to get the people around the fire to quit accusing him of having been with Jesus. Peter denied Him three times. The third time it says he began to cuss and swear (see Matthew 26:74). So they quit calling him a disciple of Jesus. He'd been around Jesus so long, he was just acting so much like Him that they started picking up on it. "This man, he acts like Jesus." After he got saved and converted and filled with the Holy Ghost, they started accusing him and he rose up in the power of God. They took note that these men had been with Jesus Christ (see Acts 4:13).

People do take note: "These people are Christian. They are living different. They are not perfect. But boy, I'll tell you what. They are quick to repent, quick to believe. They're sold out to God. When they went to the altar, they got it. When they went down under the water, they came back up new." This is what Paul says in Titus 2 about looking for the blessed hope and glorious appearance of Jesus. He goes on, "Jesus Christ, who gave himself for us, that he might redeem us from all iniquity and purifying to himself, a peculiar people, zealous of good works" (v 14 KJV). Are you zealous of good works? Are you as excited about living for God as you were the first day that you gave Him your heart and life? Are you excited about the church? Are you excited about witnessing to somebody? Are you excited about telling somebody about Jesus and inviting them to church? Are you excited about reading your Bible? Are you excited about praying? Are you excited about coming to church and lifting up hands and praising God and thanking Him for what He's doing? That's what you're supposed to be.

Work out your salvation. Make sure every day of your life. Somebody might say, "Oh, I don't think you need to be that strong with it." You might debate me, but what about the apostle Paul? Look in Colossians 1 and see what the apostle Paul has to say. "And he is the head of the body, the church: who is the beginning, the firstborn from the dead; that in all things he might have the preeminence" (Colossians 1:18 KJV). He's the first born from the dead. He's the head of the church. He has preeminence. What does that mean? He's got the final word. When I ask Jesus to be my Lord, He's the final word.

"For it pleased the Father that in him should all fullness dwell; And, having made peace through the blood of his cross, by him to reconcile all things unto himself; by him, I say, whether they be things in earth, or things in heaven" (vv 19-20 KJV). Jesus came and brought everything back to God. He reconciled us, brought us back in harmony with God.

"And you, that were sometime alienated and enemies in your mind by wicked works, yet now hath He reconciled in the body of His flesh through death, to present you holy and unblameable and unreprovable in His sight" (vv 21-22 KJV).

You sinners were lost and without hope. But Jesus came to reconcile you who were enemies to God and in your sin, to bring you back to God and make you holy and without blame, lovable and godly in God's sight. God could look on you and say, "That's mine. That's my child." That's you and me that were sometime alienated, separated from God, without access to God, enemies to God. But now it doesn't matter what the devil says about you. God's not going to side with him against you. He's with you. Being holy, unblameable, and unreprovable in the sight of God is what happens when I make Jesus Lord. When I get saved, I get in God's presence and He's on my side. The accuser of the brethren can come in and say what he wants to. God says, "Shut up. He belongs to me and is sealed by the blood of the lamb. He was an enemy to me, but now he's my friend. He was alienated from me, but now we're one together." Now my Bible doesn't have a period after "sight" in verse 22. So he's adding something to this; verse 23 is added after verse 22. "If ye continue in faith grounded and settled, and be not moved away from the hope of the Gospel, which ye have heard, and which was preached to every creature which is under heaven, whereof I, Paul am made a minister" (v 23 KJV).

If? That's right. There's a condition? "I thought I could just get saved any old way, and I could get in heaven any old way. Because after all, I'm saved: I don't have to go to church, read my Bible. I don't have to live a certain way. God understands." Not according to the apostle Paul. He says "if you continue in the faith," so that means I can get out of this, I can forfeit this. Even though I ask Jesus in my heart, I still have a free will.

If you continue in the faith, "grounded and settled and be not moved away from the hope of the Gospel," what hope? Titus 2 says the blessed hope of the return of the Lord Jesus Christ.

There's more to salvation than this going to the altar and kneeling down. There's more to this new birth than just saying Jesus is Lord and then living any way. God expects not just a confession, but a commitment. God demands and expects out of us more than a confession. It's time we get holy and live for God.

I want to conclude this chapter with Luke 14. Jesus is tying this in with where the master told his servant in verse 23 to "go out into the highways and hedges, and compel them to come in, that my house may be filled" (KJV). He tells him who the all are that can come into his house and fill it. He says in verse 26, "If any man come to me, and hate not his father, and mother, and wife, and children, and brethren, and sisters, yea, and his own life also, he cannot be my disciple" (KJV). The word translated "hate" there, if you study it out, means "prefer." Let's say it like this so it makes a little more sense to us: "If any man come to me and prefer his father and mother and wife and children and brethren and sisters, yea, and his own life also, he cannot be my disciple." He is saying, "If you come to me, but put anybody in front of me, you can't be my disciple."

I love Mom and Dad, but they're not going to keep me out of heaven. I love my wife and children, but they aren't going to keep me out of heaven. I love my friends and family, but they're not going to keep me from serving the Lord. I don't care if they all stand around the house and laugh at me because I'm a fanatic. I don't care. I am not going to prefer them above my Lord and Savior. I love them. I'll pray for them and help them. I won't treat them spitefully but I'm not going to let them dominate my life and keep me from serving the Lord Jesus with all my heart.

"And whosoever doth not bear his cross, and come after me, cannot be my disciple" (Luke 14:27 KJV). What's does it mean to bear the cross? What did Jesus do on the cross? He died. Paul said to the Corinthians that he died daily (see 1 Corinthians 15:31).

He says anybody who's not willing to crucify their flesh and deny the world—the flesh, the lust, the pride of life, and the junk—and follow Him daily is not worthy of Him.

Salvation was not a one-time trip to the altar to get up and live the rest of your life any old way you want to live it. Salvation is a daily commitment to Jesus Christ. You were born again. You were introduced into the kingdom of God one time, but salvation is a commitment every day of your life.

Jesus is still talking about compelling them to come into the master's house when He says, "For which of you, intending to build a tower, sitteth not down first, and counteth the cost, whether he have sufficient to finish it? Lest haply, after he hath laid the foundation, and is not able to finish it, all that behold it begin to mock him, Saying, This man began to build, and was not able to finish." (Luke 14:28-30 KJV). He's still talking about salvation. He's saying, "You ought to sit down and count the cost. You ought to realize it's going to cost you something. It's going to cost you some effort.

It's going to cost you some commitment." "Or what king, going to make war against another king, sitteth not down first, and consulteth whether he be able with ten thousand to meet him that cometh against him with twenty thousand? Or else, while the other is yet a great way off, he sendeth an ambassage, and desireth conditions of peace. So likewise, whosoever he be of you that forsaketh not all that he hath, he cannot be my disciple" (Luke 14:31-22 KJV).

That doesn't mean you've got to sell your house, give up your clothes, give your car away and live with the shirt and pants you got on you and that's all, or go off to a mission field someplace. But that means that you are going to have to put your desires and plans in the hands of God and say, every day, "Jesus, you are Lord of my life. And there isn't anything more important in my life than Jesus Christ."

Somebody may say, "I don't know if I can make it or finish." That's a cop out; that is just an excuse to live in your sin. Nobody knows they can finish until they make a commitment to finish.

God is not saying, "Sit down and use this as an excuse not to get saved." He's saying, "When you get saved, make a full 100% commitment to finish this thing. Don't just be a starter, be a finisher!"

"Salt is good: but if the salt have lost his savour, wherewith shall it be seasoned? It is neither fit for the land, nor yet for the dunghill; but men cast it out. He that hath ears to hear, let him hear" (Luke 14:34-35 KJV).

What happens to people that come to the altar and let sin dominate their lives, not following after God? The world tramples on them. Another place says salt that lost its flavor is not good for anything except to be trampled under the feet of men (see Matthew 5:13). When the salt would lose its saltiness, they couldn't use it for anything. They'd take that old salt and they'd sprinkle it on the steps. Hopefully, it melted some of the ice and it got walked upon by the feet of the people. It wasn't any good for anything else. They just put it on the walks, trying to keep the walks clear.

He's saying that when we don't make a full commitment to God, we allow the devil to steal from us and rob from us. He's saying the world will come in and trample you with drugs, alcohol, sex, money, and deals and this and that. They are trying to get you to compromise so they can trample you under their feet. I refuse to be trampled under the feet of the world. I am not going to lose my saltiness for the world. I'm not going to compromise my walk with God for the world. I'm saved today. I'm going to be saved tomorrow. If I make a mistake, before they can throw me out under their feet, I'm going to repent and get my life right with God. I'm going to be saved. I choose to make Jesus Lord of my life. That's true salvation.

When we choose salvation, we enter the inheritance of God because the Bible says that when we make Jesus Lord, God becomes our father and we become

His children. We become one spirit with the Lord, and God Himself delivers us from the power of darkness and translates us over into the kingdom of the Son of God and makes us partakers of the inheritance of the saints in life. But if we don't stick with God, we will not partake of our inheritance. We'll be trampled under the enemies feet.

I want to challenge you to make the commitment. I challenge you to count the cost. I challenge you to deny ungodliness and worldliness. I challenge you to be zealous for the things of God.

Prayer to Receive Jesus as Savior and Lord

Dear God in Heaven,

I come to You to make sure proof of my salvation. According to Romans 10:9-10, "That if you confess with your mouth the Lord Jesus and believe in your heart that God has raised Him from the dead, you will be saved. For with the heart one believes unto righteousness, and with the mouth confession is made unto salvation." I come to You believing that Jesus Christ died on the cross for my sins and that You raised Him up for my justification. I open my heart and invite Jesus to come in and be my personal Lord and Savior. Lord Jesus, forgive me for all my sins and cleanse me from all unrighteousness. I believe in my heart and confess with my mouth that Jesus is now my Lord, that God raised Him from the dead and I am now saved. Thank you, Heavenly Father for receiving me into the family of God and giving me eternal salvation. I receive my salvation in Christ and declare that I am now a new creation in Christ and Jesus is my Lord! Amen!

CHAPTER 3

FOLLOWING JESUS IN BAPTISM

"And He said to them, 'Go into all the world and preach the gospel to every creature. He who believes and is baptized will be saved; but he who does not believe will be condemned" (Mark 16:15-16 NKJV).

The Lord Jesus is speaking to His disciples, telling them to go everywhere and preach the gospel to every person. Now that is good news. Everybody has the right to hear the gospel. Here's something else you need to understand. He gave that Great Commission to the church. He gave it to believers. He didn't tell angels to go in all the world and preach the gospel. He told people to go in all the world. You and I have a responsibility to be carriers of the gospel of the Lord Jesus Christ.

You cannot tithe, give offerings, give missions offerings and evangelistic offerings, and abdicate yourself from your responsibility of going ahead and carrying it yourself. You're supposed to tithe. You're supposed to give offerings and missionary offerings, and you should sow into evangelistic organizations, but that does not exempt you from being a carrier of the gospel yourself.

I cannot just give and say, "Well, I've done my part." Some people say, "Well, I'm praying. I'm not really good at going out." You can pray, and you should pray, but you cannot pray and then not go out. "Well, I'm not called to preach." But He didn't say that you had to be called to preach. He said you had to go out and tell people. Preach just means to proclaim, to bring forth the proclamation or to declare.

Every believer has been given the privilege and the responsibility of taking the gospel of the Lord Jesus Christ to the lost and hurting. Every person. The Lord said in Matthew 9:38: "Therefore pray the Lord of the harvest to send out laborers into His harvest" (NKJV). The Amplified Classic translation said to force him out, thrust him into the harvest field. We ought to be praying, "Lord, stir up your lazy Christians and send them out to people and let them tell the testimony that Jesus is alive. "If we are ever going to grow and reach out to our world and make an impact, we're going to have to tell people about Jesus. Some people think, "I don't know what to say." But if you'll just tell them what God did for you, it'll be a good thing.

Remember in Mark 5 when Jesus went to the country of the Gadarenes and ministered to the demonic man. He cast the legion of demons out of the man, and the man wanted to follow Him. He said, "No, just go tell everybody what great things God has done for you" (see v 19). He didn't have any word. He just went out and told his testimony: "Here's what God did for me. And He'll do it for you."

Those people asked Jesus to leave, but you read a couple of chapters later when the Lord Jesus went back to that area. When they heard it was Jesus back on their coast, they went out and got people everywhere and brought them and put them at His feet. They hoped He'd heal them too. That old boy did a pretty good job. He didn't have a Bible. He hadn't gone to Bible school. The only lesson he learned was from Jesus. The only lesson that Jesus taught him was "go tell everybody what great things God has done for you."

We're not to hide our testimony under a bushel. We're not to hide it and keep it away. Every opportunity you get, when somebody says, "Boy, you're doing good," you need to say, "Yeah, let me tell you why." Or they say, "Well, you're looking good today. What's with you?" Just put a smile on your face and tell them, "Glory to God. I'm a new creature. Jesus is my Lord; I'm going to heaven someday."

Brother Hagin told the story of how when he first got up from his bed of affliction, he carried a New Testament around with him and he'd walk up to somebody and say, "I'm a new creature." They'd look at him and say, "You're a what?"

He'd say, "Yeah, I'm a new creature. Let me show you." He would turn over to 2 Corinthians 5:17: "Therefore if any man be in Christ, he is a new creature: old things are passed away; behold, all things are become new" (KJV). He said, "I'm a new creature in Christ Jesus. Old things have passed away. All things become new. You know, you can be one too."

It's easy to witness. It's easy to testify, but here's something you need to remember. Some of you have gotten used to coming to church. We have gotten wrapped up and tied up in going to church: it's natural to us. It's not a natural thing to everyone. I remember when my daughter Anna was a teenager. Some of her friends came over and were visiting with her. They came to church with her, and I noticed they were excited to come, but they were a little apprehensive. It was a different thing. I knew they went to church, but maybe they didn't go as much as Anna did. We just raised her up in church. When your daddy's a preacher, you go to church. So it was a very natural thing for her to go to church. But I was watching, and I remember thinking, "Man, that reminds me of me back when I first gave my heart to the Lord."

Do you remember when you first even got saved and Wednesday night would roll around and there was a battle going on all the time: we'll go to church, not go to church, stay home, go, I'm tired? Or Sunday morning rolled around, and you could get up at six o'clock in the morning all week long, but on Sunday morning, it's the hardest thing. We need to be aware of that. You need to be conscious of that. When you share with people, you've got to be conscious of the fact that the enemy's out there trying to pull them down. The enemy's trying to hinder them, and we need to love people and just share with them the good news and help them to know that Jesus will be patient with them. Be upbeat and kind and just make it so inviting that they want to come and praise God. They'll want to have in their life what you have in yours.

But Jesus said, "Go into all the world and preach the gospel to every creature. He who believes and is baptized will be saved; but he who does not believe will be condemned" (Mark 16:15-16 NKJV). He said, "You're either going accept it and get saved, or you're going to reject it and you'll be condemned." Notice He said, "Believe and be baptized." I want to touch on those two things.

First of all, what are we going to believe? We've got to believe the gospel. What is the gospel? We need to learn what we're believing. If we're going to believe something, let's find out what we're believing. First Corinthians 15:1-4 says, "Moreover, brethren, I declare to you the gospel which I preached to you, which also you received and in which you stand, by which also you are saved, if you hold fast that word which I preached to you—unless you believed in vain. For I delivered to you first of all that which I also received: that Christ died for our sins according to the Scriptures, and that He was buried, and that He rose again the third day according to the Scriptures" (NKJV).

Paul says you received the gospel and now you're standing in the gospel. The gospel's not something you hear one time and you walk away and say, "I got it." No, you hear it. You stand in it; you believe it. You walk in it. Then he says the gospel will save you if you stick with it. I don't believe you can run to the altar and say, "Jesus, be my Lord," and stay in church for a couple of weeks and then go out and live like the devil the rest of your life and go to heaven. I don't believe it's a possibility. The church world has preached "God loves you." He does love you, but He also expects you to love Him and give your life to Him just as He is giving His life to you.

Paul basically says, "Here's the gospel that I preach to you, that you received and if you stand in it you'll be saved by it if you'll keep it in memory, if you'll stick with it." What is the gospel Paul taught? That Christ died for our sins. "According to the Scriptures," what's that mean? Second Corinthians 5:21 says He was made to be sin for us who knew no sin. First Peter 2:24 says, "who Himself bore our sins in His own body on the tree, that we, having died to sins, might live for righteousness" (NKJV). John 1:29 says, "Behold! The Lamb of God who takes away the sin of the world!" (NKJV). Jesus became our substitute. He died in our place. He took our sin. According to Scripture, Jesus paid the price for our sin.

Then Paul says that He was buried. We've got to believe that they took Jesus Christ down off the cross and buried Him in that tomb, and He arose again on the third day. We've got to believe that on the third day, on that Easter First Fruits morning, that Jesus arose from the grave. As the lamb of God that was slain from the foundation of the world, He arose as the Lord, high priest of the church. He arose as your Savior, as your Lord, your healer, your baptizer, your friend that sticks closer than a brother. We've got to believe that Jesus is exactly who the Bible says He is.

He's not coming back the second time as a suffering savior. He's coming back as the conquering King of Kings and Lord of Lords. You've got to understand Jesus will never suffer another sin. He'll never suffer another heartache. He'll never suffer another oppressive thing. He'll never suffer another curse. He'll never have to lay aside His glory. He'll never have to take off His crown again. He'll never have to change. He has done all that He needs to do for you and me to walk in salvation and victory forever. Paul told the Corinthians that you need to remember this is the gospel. This saves you. You need to stay with Him when it looks like you can't make it. Stick with it. When the devil says, "It ain't worth it," stick with it. Whenever the pressures of life are coming in, stick with it because if you'll stick with it, it'll stick with you. God will stand right by your side, and He'll get you through.

You might say, "Well, I believe all of that so what about me?" First you need to know that Bible *believing* and today's church's *believing* are two different things. In today's church, *believing* means "I agree with it?" But Bible *believing* is more than just agreeing with it. Believing in the Bible is an action verb. It means doing something about it. People today say, "Well, I believe in God." That doesn't mean anything. They're still dying in their sins and going to hell because the devils believe and tremble at His name (see James 2:19). You can go to church; devils go to church. Sometimes I believe churches are more full of the devil than they are anything else. The devil goes to church.

In Job, all the sons of God were coming and worshiping God. The devil came too and accused Job.

Just believing churchy or religious believing is not enough. Bible believing means you act upon it. It means you do something about it. It means you reach out and grab ahold of it. You attain it. If I believe that Jesus died, according to the Scriptures, for my sins and was buried and the third day He arose from the dead, then I need to do something about that. Romans 10:9-10 tells me what to do: "that if you confess with your mouth the Lord Jesus and believe in your heart that God has raised Him from the dead, you will be saved. For with the heart one believes unto righteousness, and with the mouth confession is made unto salvation" (NKJV). He didn't say you had to do penance for a year.

He didn't say you had to redo everything in your past. He just said you've got to believe: Jesus died for your sin. God raised Him from the dead. Believe He's Lord and accept Him in your heart and confess Him with your mouth.

Then in verse 10, he is talking about repentance. True repentance is making a declaration that I believe that Jesus is Lord and that He died for my sins so that I don't have to be under condemnation or guilt. I don't have to live a defeated life. I don't have to hold my head down. Sin no longer has dominion over me because Jesus conquered death, hell, and the grave.

He conquered sin for me. He took my sins. I don't have to have it. You can say, "Jesus, come into my heart. I receive you as my Lord. I confess you now as my Lord. And according to the Scriptures, I'm a new creation in Christ Jesus. Old things have passed while all things become new. I am now a child of the living God." That's believing on the gospel.

The Lord told the disciples to go preach the gospel. That's the gospel: if you'll believe that Jesus died for you, that God raised Him from the dead, and that He is Lord and act upon that and confess with your mouth that Jesus is Lord. Then of course, Matthew 10 says you've got to confess Him before people and you can't be ashamed of Him. We cannot just confess Jesus is Lord in the church, and you can't just confess Jesus is Lord when everything's easy and everything's good. You need to confess Jesus is Lord in the crisis of your life. When all of hell is breaking loose against you, you need to confess Jesus is Lord. When it doesn't look like it's working in your life, you need to confess to those who are skeptical and those who are persecuting you. You need to still confess, "Jesus is still my Lord."

Job said, "Though He slay me, yet will I trust in Him" (NKJV). That's a powerful statement. When a man sitting there covered from the top of his head to the soles of his feet with boils, in ashes and sackcloth; and he's lost all his family, lost all his money, lost all his friends; and he's got three guys sitting there telling him what a bad person he is, that's a pretty good confession, isn't it? We need to make that kind of stand. That's the kind of commitment God's looking for today. That's the kind of commitment that brings revival. A fanatic is somebody that'll fight you for what they believe. We need to be fanatical for Jesus, but we need to know what we believe and what we're fanatical about.

So the first part of this is believe, but the second part was He said to be baptized. I want you to see that baptism is important. We could go through various Scriptures throughout the Bible, and we could show you how the early church was quick to baptize people. It was an important ordinance. They put great importance to it, but baptism within itself, just the physical act of water, will not get you saved. You need to know that if you're putting your faith in a baptism—that you're going to get to heaven because you got water baptized—you're going to be greatly shocked when you stand before the Lord someday.

I'm going to prove it to you. "For Christ also suffered once for sins, the just for the unjust, that He might bring us to God, being put to death in the flesh but made alive by the Spirit, by whom also He went and preached to the spirits in prison, who formerly were disobedient, when once the Divine long-suffering waited in the days of Noah, while the ark was being prepared, in which a few, that is, eight souls, were saved through water. " (1 Peter 3:18-20 NKJV).

Now notice there Peter says that the Lord died for us, and down in the prison gates of the earth, He preached to those that have gone on before. He preached to all those that had died down into the quarters of hell itself. He preached and told them, "I am the Christ. I'm the one that was prophesied." Then He arose victorious.

But then he's talking about eight souls saved by water. In other words, just like water saved Noah, baptism saves us now, the first part of verse 21 says. A lot of people stop right there and try to build a church doctrine. "See, you got to be baptized before you are saved. It's baptism that saves us." No, no, no. You can take half a Scripture out of one setting, put it with another half a Scripture from another setting and make any kind of doctrine you want to have, but it wouldn't be right. You can read over in Acts where it says that when Judas found out that he couldn't get set free, he went out and hanged himself. Then you can go over in Luke where the Lord was talking about the good Samaritan and He said, "Go down and do likewise." You could take those two Scriptures put them together and say, "Judas went out and hanged himself; go down and do likewise" and preach people should go out and hang themselves. You might say, "Well, that's crazy." It's no more crazy than this.

I heard a fellow one time say that he read down in Acts 2:1-4: "And when the day of Pentecost was fully come, they were all with one accord in one place. And suddenly there came a sound from heaven as of a rushing mighty wind, and it filled all the house where they were sitting. And there appeared unto them cloven tongues like as of fire, and it sat upon each of them. And they were all filled with the Holy Ghost." (KJV). He stopped right there. He said, "That's all we need to read. Nothing else is vital or important about this. We just want to show you that you need to be filled with the Holy Ghost." I thought, "You can't stop there in the middle of a verse; that's like getting halfway in an intersection and stopping right under the red light.

You've got to go through that intersection. I mean, you're going to block traffic all four directions if you get out in the middle of the intersection and then stop. No, you need to read all that verse."

"And they were all filled with the Holy Ghost and began to speak in other tongues, as the Spirit gave them utterance" (Acts 2:4 KJV).

It's the same thing here in 1 Peter 3. You've got to read verse 21 in its entirety. "The like figure to this, even baptism, doth also now save us (not the putting away of the filth of the flesh, but the answer of a good conscience toward God) by the resurrection of Jesus Christ" (KJV). What he's saying is that just the physical act of baptism in water will not save you. Baptism must be in accordance with the washing of the sin from your conscience, from your spirit. So baptism as an act in itself will not save you. But baptism is to be included in your salvation experience. As you make Jesus Lord, you are to follow Him in the ordinance given to the church to be baptized in water. They work together.

I found this to be true. Anybody who didn't get enough salvation to get water baptized didn't stay in the church very long. We need to be born again in our spirit, and then we need to be baptized.

In Acts 8, Philip went down to Samaria and preached the gospel to the multitudes. There was great joy in the city. In verse 12, it says when they believed the word, they were all baptized, both men and women. They followed the scriptural example. Then Philip is told to go down to Gaza down in the desert (v 26), and there he meets up with a eunuch from Ethiopia who is reading from Isaiah

53. "So Philip ran to him, and heard him reading the prophet Isaiah, and said, 'Do you understand what you are reading?'" (v 30 NKJV).

Notice this response. Here's why it's so important that you and I learn the Scriptures and witness to people. "How can I, unless some man guide me?" (v 31 NKJV). How am I going to believe on God and get saved if somebody doesn't come and tell me how to get it?

There are people wanting to be saved. There are people seeking the truth, but how shall they find the truth without somebody coming and guiding them into it? You and I have been given the Great Commission. He's saying, "I need somebody to explain to me how to get saved and somebody to care enough about me to tell me the truth."

Philip sat down beside him and "The place in the Scripture which he read was this: "He was led as a sheep to the slaughter; And as a lamb before its shearer is silent, So He opened not His mouth. In His humiliation His justice was taken away, And who will declare His generation? For His life is taken from the earth.' So the eunuch answered Philip and said, 'I ask you, of whom does the prophet say this, of himself or of some other man?'" (vv 32-34 NKJV).

In other words, "What's he talking about? Who is this? Who's he talking about?" Verse 35 says, "Then Philip opened his mouth, and beginning at this same Scripture, preached Jesus to him." (NKJV). If you don't know anything else, just preach Jesus. Just tell them it's Jesus.

You don't need to know anything but Jesus; the name of Jesus will get you saved. It's not how much you read. It's not what church you belong to. It's Jesus. He's the one who's going to get you saved. You need to look to Him. "Now as they went down the road, they came to some water. And the eunuch said, 'See, here is water. What hinders me from being baptized?'" (v 36 NKJV). They came up to a water hole and the eunuch looks to Philip, who's been preaching to him. He says, "Here's water." Apparently, he's preaching baptism.

The man knows a little something. Philip must be saying you've got to believe and repent and be baptized. Isn't that what they said in Acts 2:38 on the day of Pentecost? The people said, "Brother, what must we do?" Peter stood up and said to repent and be baptized to receive the gift of the Holy Ghost.

Philip was there. He heard that. So he's preaching that you've got to repent, give your life to God, and be baptized. The man asks what hinders him from being baptized. We could say it like this: What would qualify me for the right to be baptized? Isn't that saying the same thing? Isn't that saying it in a way we can understand? What do I need to do before I can become a qualified candidate to be baptized in water?

What condition must I meet to be baptized in water? That's what he's saying. That's what we've got to ask.

In verse 37, Philip said, "If you believe with all your heart, you may" (NKJV). What qualifies me to have the right to go down into that water and be baptized? I've got to believe on the Lord Jesus Christ. I've got to have something on the inside of me working. The man answered, "I believe that Jesus Christ is the Son of God" (v 37 NKJV). He followed Romans 10:10: I believe that Jesus Christ is the son of God. I confess that Jesus Christ is Lord. The moment he confessed Jesus is Lord, he became qualified to get baptized.

If he didn't confess Jesus is Lord, he was not qualified to get baptized. You've got to be born again or you must become a believer to be baptized. It said that he believed and then was baptized. You've got to believe first and then you follow through. Now let's look at the next thing here. Verse 38 says, "So he commanded the chariot to stand still. And both Philip and the eunuch went down into the water, and he baptized him" (NKJV). Here's something about baptism you need to see. They went down into the water for baptism. Every scholar, every one of the church fathers, all the Greek scholars that I've read and studied after say baptism means to be immersed, to be taken under, to be taken down under and brought up. They went down into the water. He was baptized, and they came back out of the water. He didn't sprinkle him. He was baptized. We should do that. You might ask, "Well, why?" I believe that we need to be a stickler for the Word. Let's do it God's way, not the religious way, not man's way.

Also, you can't baptize yourself. You need somebody to help you. Who should baptize you? Somebody called and anointed of God. You don't want Joe from down at Joe's Bar and Grill baptizing you. I want somebody that's got the real deal to lay their hands on me. You come forward in church. In Luke 11:13, God says through the Lord Jesus, "If you then, being evil, know how to give good gifts to your children, how much more will your heavenly Father give the Holy Spirit to those who ask Him!" (NKJV). But you've got to be in the right place asking the right way. I wouldn't want to be out in one of these flake places.

Brother Hagin was sharing about a lady who went down to this so-called deliverance ministry. She said that when she was down there, she began to have a foam come out of her mouth. She was a good Christian. After six months, she came to a meeting he was in and met with him. She kept the tissue in her mouth all the time. She said, "I go through a box of tissue and it just runs out of my mouth. I went to this deliverance ministry, and they prayed for me and said I had a demon. After I left, this stuff started coming out of my mouth. Do you know what it is?" He said, "Yeah, you went to a deliverance ministry and got a demon." As a Christian, you can't be demon possessed but you can be physically and mentally oppressed by a demon. She was oppressed in her body by this unclean spirit.

He said, "I know exactly what to do. I can get you set free, but you're going to have to agree to do what I tell you." She says, "Anything." He said, "You've got to agree to go in the Word, stay in the Word, and get into a good church where they preach the gospel. Don't go off in these flaky meetings and get something stupid anymore." She said, "You get me set free, and I'll never go to another one of those types of flaky meetings." He just pointed his finger and said, "In the name of Jesus, you leave," and it left her and she was delivered and set free.

You don't want just anybody baptizing you in water. You don't want just anybody praying for you to get the Holy Ghost. You don't want just anybody trying to get you set free from an oppression. You don't want to go to just any place. I want to see some fruit.

You can tell me you are an apple tree all day long, but you might be a crabapple tree. I may not want your apples. If I take a bite of your fruit, I might get a stomachache. I want something good.

Philip was anointed of God. He ministered to the eunuch. You can't baptize yourself. You need someone anointed of God to baptize you. Why do you need somebody called and anointed by the Spirit of God to baptize you? They don't necessarily have to be called to preach. I would always want to get with somebody who has a calling upon their life. Someone filled with the Spirit, somebody anointed of God: why should I have somebody like that baptize me? Because baptism is an outward testimony or a witness of the inward working of God's grace that has already taken place in you.

Why do I need to be baptized properly? Why do I need to do it the way God says? Why do I need to believe? What is baptism? It is death, burial, and resurrection.

That's what water baptism is. The symbolism of it is death, burial, and resurrection. Being dead to the old man. I died with Christ. I'm buried with Christ. I'm raised up with Christ. I will show it to you in Romans 6:3-5: "Or do you not know that as many of us as were baptized into Christ Jesus were baptized into His death? Therefore we were buried with Him through baptism into death, that just as Christ was raised from the dead by the glory of the Father, even so we also should walk in newness of life. For if we have been united together in the likeness of His death, certainly we also shall be in the likeness of His resurrection" (NKJV). He's saying that Jesus was raised up by the glory of the Father.

Romans 8:11 says, "But if the Spirit of Him who raised Jesus from the dead dwells in you, He who raised Christ from the dead will also give life to your mortal bodies through His Spirit who dwells in you." (NKJV). He says the Spirit raised Jesus up in Romans 8, and in Romans 6:4, he says that Jesus was raised up by the glory of the Father. So the Holy Ghost is the glory of God. The Lord Jesus was not raised from the dead in His own accord or by His own power or might. He was raised up from the dead by the power and the glory of God coming upon Him and lifting Him up out of the dead. God the Father, by the power of the Holy Spirit, lifted Jesus up from the grave and raised Him up and seated Him in heavenly places.

Why do you need to be in the right setting? Because you are following the act of baptism and you are signifying to the world that "as Jesus died to sin, I have now died to sin. I am being buried. I cannot get myself out of this watery grave. I need the help of someone else to lift me back up." That's why you allow the person to take you down and bring you back up. You're signifying "I cannot receive this eternal life in my own accord, by my own actions. I'm helpless in my own self, but one greater than me has raised me up and made me to sit in heavenly places in Christ Jesus. Just like Jesus no longer has to die anymore to sin, and He's been buried to sin, Roman 6:11 says, likewise, I reckon myself to be dead indeed to sin, but also alive to God through Jesus Christ, my Lord. Just like I was buried with Him, now I'm raised up and I walk up out of that water saying I'm walking out of my old life into my new life. Never again will I look back, but I will walk on with God from this day forth to live the resurrected life of the Lord Jesus Christ."

The Bible says that we are washed by the washing of the water of the Word (see Ephesians 5:26). So you go down dry, but you come up wet. What he is saying there is the symbolism: "I was dry and destitute and I was unclean. But when I died in Christ, my sins were washed away and now I'm no longer a dry, dead, destitute individual. I am washed by the washing of the Word. The love, the anointing, and the power of God saturated me. Now I'm different." This is what baptism is all about. This is what the new birth is all about. This is the ordinance that the Lord gave the church, to preach this gospel, to have people believe on this gospel, to accept Jesus as Lord and then follow Him through baptism so that the world would see that I'm no longer what I used to be or who I used to be. I am a new creation in Christ. Every believer everywhere in all the world should be born again and baptized in water and then filled also with the Holy Ghost.

I will share with you one last Scripture on this subject: "And Jesus came and spoke to them, saying, "All authority has been given to Me in heaven and on earth. Go therefore and make disciples of all the nations, baptizing them in the name of the Father and of the Son and of the Holy Spirit, teaching them to observe all things that I have commanded you; and lo, I am with you always, even to the end of the age." (Matthew 28:18-20 NKJV).

Aren't you glad Jesus is the one in authority? He has all power. He is Lord. You need to get a hold of that. Jesus is Lord. Not your circumstances, not the devil, not your problems. Jesus is Lord. The thing you're facing is not all powerful. Jesus is all powerful, but now look what the Lord did with this power. He delegated that authority and power to the church. We have the awesome privilege of being able to walk in His power, glory, and anointing. As believers, we can walk in the authority of the Lord Jesus Christ and what we are to do with that authority is to teach the nations and baptize them. Now we get some controversy here because in the book of Acts they baptize in the name of the Lord, and of course, Colossians 3:17 says whatever you do in word or deed, you always do everything in the name of the Lord Jesus. But here He says to baptize in the name of the Father. If you were to study the Greek out—I'm not a Greek scholar, but I can read what Greek scholars say.

The Amplified Classic Bible, along with several other translations, reads this way: "Go then and make disciples of all the nations, baptizing them into the name of the Father and of the Son and of the Holy Spirit."

The scripturally correct way is to say baptizing them into the name of the Father, Son, and Holy Ghost. One, we're baptizing you or immersing you or bringing you into a full fellowship with the full Godhead. You're in fellowship with God the Father; you're in fellowship with God the Son; you're in fellowship with God the Holy Ghost.

Some people say, "I believe you ought to just baptize in the name of Jesus only. And that's it. Nothing else." I don't agree. The other side says, "I believe you're supposed to say in the name of the Father, Son, Holy Ghost. And that's it." No, I disagree. I believe we should do all things in the name of the Lord Jesus. I believe we should baptize in the name of Jesus, just like they did in the book of Acts. How should I do it? I believe we should do this. I believe we should say something along these lines. After a person has rendered a confession of Jesus's lordship, we should say this: "Father, I thank you for saving this individual. I thank you that you've washed him by the blood of the lamb and they're a new creation in Christ Jesus. And now upon the confession of your faith in Jesus for the remission of your sins, in the name of the Lord Jesus, I now baptize you into the Father, the Son, and the Holy Ghost."

Then I believe we've done everything the Bible tells us to do. When we run water into the baptistry and we bring people forward and baptize, we always push the drain at the end. I always tell them, "When that water's gone, it's washed all that junk away. You can't find it anymore. Tomorrow when you come in here, that place will be empty. And every time the devil comes and says, 'Well, you don't have it and you didn't make it,' you just need to say, 'Wait a minute, devil, your place is empty. It's washed, it's gone. I'm clean. I'm out of here. Jesus is my Lord.'"

Chapter 4

Being Filled with the Holy Spirit

"And He opened their understanding, that they might comprehend the Scriptures. Then He said to them, "Thus it is written, and thus it was necessary for the Christ to suffer and to rise from the dead the third day, and that repentance and remission of sins should be preached in His name to all nations, beginning at Jerusalem. And you are witnesses of these things." (Luke 24:45- 48 NKJV).

The Lord Jesus is speaking to His disciples, and He's giving the disciples their mandate. He's giving them their commission: "This is what your vision is. This is what your job description is. This is what I'm calling you to do. I have raised you up. I have opened your understanding. I have caused you to walk as my disciples. Now you have seen my resurrection.

You've seen the power of that resurrection, and now I've called you to be witnesses."

The word "witness" here doesn't just mean somebody who can go out and tell somebody. The word "witness" here means somebody who can go out and give proof. He said, "You are witnesses of these things. You are to go out and give evidential proof that I am resurrected from the dead." What He is saying to them is this: "If people will receive your witness, if they'll receive what you're telling them by both signs and wonders and word of mouth, their sins will get remitted." That's the way the disciples are supposed to go. You've got to go out and tell people, but you've also got to go out and show people and demonstrate the power of the resurrection. He said, "If they'll receive it, I'll wipe their sins out and they'll get born again, just like you." That's the Great Commission to the church.

If you want to get right down to it, He said that we are to go out to all the world and make disciples. A disciple is a follower of the teachings of his master. The trouble with the church is we've been trying to make converts. But Jesus didn't say, "Go make converts." If somebody comes up to you and says, "Would you like to get saved and go to heaven? Because if you don't get saved, you'll not go to heaven. You'll go to hell," how much intelligence does it take to make a decision? I want to go to heaven. I don't want to go to hell.

We've gone into the world and done exactly opposite of what the Lord Jesus told the disciples to do. He said, "I've opened your understanding to realize that you're going to have to have a change of heart. Your sins have to be remitted. I want you to go in all the world and make disciples. I want you to be a witness of my resurrection so that the people will believe that I am Lord. Not just believe that they're going to heaven, but they'll believe that I am Lord. And when they accept my Lordship and turn their hearts to me, I'll wipe their sins away and I'll change their nature. I'll change their heart. I'll change the way they believe and act. They'll become my disciples." That's what they were told to do. That's what you and I are told to do.

I don't want you to just change your thinking. I want you to change your believing. Too many people think just because they went to church or just because their name is on the church roll that they're a Christian. "I'm a Christian just because I heard some preacher preach. I'm a Christian just because I went to an altar one night and asked God to forgive me." Just asking God to forgive you will not get you saved. You have got to believe in your heart that Jesus died for your sin and that God raised Him from the dead, and confess Him as your Lord and give your life to Him.

God is looking for disciples, doers of the Word, followers of the teaching of the master, learners of the doctrines of Jesus Christ who are applying those truths in their lives. Are we perfect? No, nobody's perfect. But we're striving for perfection. It means we're maturing in our walk toward God because we change from the inside out.

The Lord said, "Go and make disciples; go and change people's hearts; go and witness, produce evidence and proof that will change people's hearts, convict their lives, and show them that there is a real God and He loves them and that sin can be destroyed out of their lives. They can have a new walk on Earth and they can have a new heaven to go to someday."

But now look what He says in the next verse: "Behold, I send the Promise of My Father upon you; but tarry in the city of Jerusalem until you are endued with power from on high." (Luke 24:49 NKJV). He's saying, "You've got a great task. You've got a great situation; you've got to do a great job to disciple these people and bring them out of the bondage of sin and over into righteousness, to bring them out of darkness into light, to bring them over to me." Then He says, "I'm going to tell you right now, just having a burden, a commission, and a call is not enough.

Having good intentions is not enough. Just having the Word on it is not enough." The Lord said, "You've been given the commission. You've been told what you need to do. You've been told how to do it, but I'm going to tell you right now, you are not equipped to get it done.

You go into Jerusalem, and you wait there." The word "tarry" means hang out there. "Don't start this yet. Go to Jerusalem and wait upon me. Get into my presence until you are endued with power from on high." You might ask what that power is. Let's go over to Acts 1 and find out.

The same author who wrote the gospel of Luke is also the writer of the book of Acts. Luke was a physician, who became one of the disciples of the Lord Jesus Christ, and he says this: "And being assembled together with *them,* He commanded them not to depart from Jerusalem, but to wait for the Promise of the Father, "which," *He said,* "you have heard from Me; for John truly baptized with water, but you shall be baptized with the Holy Spirit not many days from now." (Acts 1:4-5 NKJV). He's saying, "Wait until you get it." Same thing, different wording. What is going to give me the ability and the power that I need to do what God has called me to do? The baptism in the Holy Ghost. I need the Holy Ghost.

He says in verse eight of this same chapter, "But ye shall receive power, after that the Holy Ghost is come upon you: and ye shall be witnesses unto me both in Jerusalem, and in all Judaea, and in Samaria, and unto the uttermost part of the earth" (v 8 KJV). The Holy Ghost is the one who empowers us to be the witness that Jesus has called us to be.

What the church has done is we've taken our Bibles and we've gone out here without any power, without any strength, without any anointing. We preached a legalistic way: "Don't do this and do this and you can get saved. Don't do this and God will bless you." We've brought people right back under the law. All we've done is made converts when we needed to get filled with the Holy Ghost and let the Spirit of God breathe life into this Bible. Then when we speak it out to people, it's no longer a book of regulations and rules and dos and don'ts, but it is a life-changing message that convinces you that Jesus Christ died on a cross almost 2,000 years ago and provided a way for you to have the eternal life and be filled with the Holy Ghost.

You may not think you need the Holy Ghost, but you need the Holy Ghost. You cannot do what God has called you to do without the Holy Ghost. It's not me who's telling you that you need the Holy Ghost. Jesus told us we need the Holy Ghost. Luke tells us we need the Holy Ghost. You need this. I don't care if you're Baptist, Methodist, or Lutheran. I don't care if you are whatever name, whatever your background is, you can just strip the label off of it and fill it with the Holy Ghost.

The Bible talks about when Moses was there on the backside of the desert. He saw a bush burning. When he walked over to it, the glory of God was there. The voice of God spoke out to him. People have tried to go back and I'm sure archaeologist have tried to figure out what kind of bush that was.

But I'm going to tell you that any old bush will do. All you've got to do is be available. God doesn't care if you are a Baptist bush, a Methodist bush, a Catholic bush: all you've got to do is get some Holy Ghost on and you'll burn and not get consumed.

If you want God to talk through you and God to move through you, you need to burn. There are all kinds of bushes sitting out there in that desert, but only one got Moses's attention. It was the one that was producing God.

You and I need to be filled with the Holy Ghost. You need the anointing of God. You need it to do what God is calling you to do. We are called to be witnesses. When Acts 1:8 says that "You shall receive power," the word "power" there means the divine enabling of God. You will have ability that is not just from natural wisdom. A divine enabling will come upon you. Things that you couldn't do before you are able to do. The ability to know Scripture that you didn't know before, the ability to speak when you couldn't speak before, the ability to be bold when you were fearful and timid before, the ability to stand up in the power and the anointing of God, which you didn't have before: that is what the baptism of the Holy Spirit is about.

You need the Holy Ghost. You need the Holy Ghost to know how to pray for your kids. You need the Holy Ghost to know how to pray for your family. You need the Holy Ghost to enable you to know how to believe God and get your needs met. All of that is witnessing.

You take somebody that's full of fear and afraid to step out, and then they get baptized with the Holy Ghost. The next time you see them, they're speaking faith. They're doing things that are beyond their ability, beyond their education, beyond their natural means. You might ask, "What happened to you?" They'll say, "I'll tell you what happened to me. The Helper came into me and He gave me boldness and introduced me to a greater revelation of Jesus Christ. I found out who I am, and He is the one enabling me to do what I'm called to do." It's the witness. It's a divine enabling. You shall receive power, the divine ability of God imparted to you. I thank God for the Holy Ghost. I've been in situations before where people have come to me for advice and counsel. As they sat there and told me their troubles, in my mind I had no answer for them. I'm sitting there thinking, "Man, these people are going to find out how unspiritual you really are here in just about a second when they get done talking." I'm keeping a calm face but my mind is in a panic.

About that time, the Holy Ghost kicks in and He begins to bring divine revelation. He begins to speak to me and show me what to say and how to help them. During these times of ministry, I just began to dig down inside of me in the Spirit of God, and all of a sudden that divine enabling kicked in and the gift of the Holy Ghost kicked in, and God began to show me things. I'd do something or say something, and then the person I was ministering to walked out of that situation on top. I would shake my head and think, "Ooh, my goodness gracious. God, you're so good." They all stood back saying, "That's one of the wisest men I ever met."

He just comes up with the most wise advice. I'm glad I'm filled with the Holy Ghost.

He takes you out of your ability over into God's ability. You don't know how to make the right decision, but the Holy Ghost does. You don't know which way to go, but the Holy Ghost does. You don't know what to say, but the Holy Ghost does. You don't know what that Scripture means, but the Holy Ghost does. You need the Holy Ghost. Every believer needs to get so full of the Holy Ghost that it just oozes out of you. He said, "When you're full of the Holy Ghost, you will be my witness. You shall receive power for that. The Holy Ghost and you shall be witnesses under me." The Holy Ghost is the one that gives you the ability to produce Jesus.

Sometimes you're there ministering and you're telling somebody about Jesus, and they're standing there shaking their head saying, "No, no, no." Your natural mind goes, "Whoa, I didn't get through that time." But later on, you hear the report coming back where they went and told somebody, "I'm telling you, when So-and-so was talking to me, the power of God was so powerful. That's all I could do to not get saved. I'm telling you what, I'm going to go get saved." You're thinking, "I didn't feel it." You didn't have to feel it. He wasn't there for you. It was for you to witness to them. It was a divine conviction that flowed out of you. It was something that you couldn't make happen in yourself. You could read a hundred Scriptures and not get done what needed to be done. But the Holy Spirit hooked up with you, and that divine personality of God flowed out of you. That power went out and witnessed while you were talking. You need that. Every believer needs that. I want the Holy Ghost. You need the Holy Spirit.

The Holy Spirit is the one that gives you that divine enabling ability to live for God. Without the Holy Spirit, you will get your head beat in, your ears boxed, your eyes beat up every time you turn around because the devil is going to whip you without the power of the Holy Spirit in your life. The Lord Jesus Christ did not even begin His ministry until He was baptized in the Jordan River and was filled with the Holy Ghost. He didn't do a miracle until He was filled with the Holy Ghost. "Jesus could do anything," you say. No, He couldn't. He left all of that in heaven. Philippians 2:7 says He came to this earth and became a servant.

He laid aside all of His glory in heaven. He came down here and took upon Himself the form of flesh and blood. He had to do it just like you and I do it. He was God incarnate—you've got to believe that to get saved—but He was humanity. You've got to believe that to do His works. Jesus did not heal people or walk on the water as God. The Lord Jesus walked on water as a man, anointed of God. He walked on water through faith.

You might wonder how I can preach that. In Matthew 14, when Peter walked out to meet Him on the water, and Peter saw the wind and waves, he became afraid and he started to sink. He cried out to Jesus, and Jesus reached out and grabbed him, lifting him up. He said, "You have little faith." The Lord was saying, "If you'd have had faith, like I've got faith, and trusted God, like I'm trusting God, you'd have walked on the water just like me and not sank." So the Lord tells us there that He was walking on water by faith in God.

When did He walk on the water? After spending all night in prayer. You go pray seven or eight hours in the Holy Ghost and see what you walk on. If you pray for about eight hours in tongues, you will get filled up and charged up and get your battery charged by the Spirit of God.

It's the Holy Spirit that gives us that ability to be overcomers in this life. He is the one that opens our understanding and makes the Word of God become real to us. In John 16:7-15, Jesus says, "Nevertheless I tell you the truth. It is to your advantage that I go away; for if I do not go away, the Helper will not come to you; but if I depart, I will send Him to you. And when He has come, He will convict the world of sin, and of righteousness, and of judgment: of sin, because they do not believe in Me; of righteousness, because I go to My Father and you see Me no more; of judgment, because the ruler of this world is judged. "I still have many things to say to you, but you cannot bear them now. However, when He, the Spirit of truth, has come, He will guide you into all truth; for He will not speak on His own authority, but whatever He hears He will speak; and He will tell you things to come. He will glorify Me, for He will take of what is Mine and declare it to you. All things that the Father has are Mine. Therefore I said that He will take of Mine and declare it to you." (NKJV).

First, aren't you glad Jesus told us the truth? The Helper is the Holy Ghost, and Jesus said "It's better, in fact, it's necessary, for me to go away. I've got a job to do, and I need to get it done. Because just as soon as I get it done, I'm going to send to you what I went for." Jesus did not just come to defeat the devil. He came to redeem mankind. He came to purchase us back. He came to bring us back into liberty. He came to bring us back into a full walk with God Almighty. The Holy Spirit is God, just like Jesus is God. He's no less God than Jesus is. He's no less God than the Father is. He proceeds out of the Father. He's a part of the Father. He is deity. He is God coming to live in you. You need the Holy Spirit because He reproves or convinces of sin because people don't believe in Jesus. The first ministry of the Holy Spirit is to bring you to Jesus.

Once He brings you to Jesus, He doesn't stop. You need to be filled with the Holy Ghost because the Holy Ghost will keep you out of sin if you'll listen to Him. When you are in sin, He'll let you know it. A lot of Christians are running around saying, "I just didn't know I was wrong." But they're lying; their heart knew it. The reason their heart knew it is because the Holy Ghost dwells on the inside of them. He was telling their heart, "That's wrong, boy." The Holy Ghost is there to reprove and correct and convince you that that's the wrong way to go; get your eyes back on Jesus. When you're getting ready to make your own decision, the Holy Spirit will help you make godly decisions, not carnal decisions.

Paul wrote in Ephesians 1:13 that when you believed on the Lord Jesus Christ, you were sealed with the promise of the Holy Spirit. The Holy Ghost comes to seal you, to keep you saved, to keep you living for God, to keep you empowered of God, and to keep your eyes on Jesus.

I thank God for the day that I made Jesus Christ my Lord and I got born again. But I also rejoice just as much for the day that I got baptized in the Holy Ghost and the divine third person of the Godhead came into me and dwelled in me in His fullness because He began to open up the Bible to me. He's the one that wrote it. The Holy Spirit is the author of the Bible. Peter and Paul both tell us that all the Scriptures are inspired or God breathed. In other words, it came by the Spirit of God. Peter says it was all given by inspiration of God.

The Holy Ghost moved on people's hearts and spoke it into them, and they wrote it down. The Spirit of God is the author of the book. If you want to know what's all the hidden secrets and all the meanings and what this word means and what that passage says, you ought to go to the one that wrote it.

The Holy Spirit is sent to help us to live in the truth of the Word of God, to walk in the victory, to keep us sealed for God, and to keep us out of sin. He gives us the ability to be an overcomer in this life. The second thing He came to do is reprove of righteousness or convince us of righteousness. The Holy Spirit is here to remind you that even though you cannot see Jesus, you are still in right standing with God.

Even though the Lord Jesus is not here in the flesh, you've got rights with God and privileges with God and you're still God's chosen. The Holy Spirit is always here working to convince you that you are right: "God loves you. He's for you. Don't listen to that lie the devil's peddling. You don't listen to that condemnation and guilt. Don't you let the devil talk. I'm here to convince you that you are the righteousness of God in Christ." You may not see it. You may not feel like it, but the Spirit of God is on the inside of you saying, "That's all right. You stand up there and you look at that situation. Say 'greater is He that's in me than he that's in the world. And I'm not coming off of my walk with God. You're not getting me out of church, devil. You're not getting me away from the believers, devil. You're not going to cause my prayers not to work, devil, because I am the righteousness of God in Christ. The Spirit of God on the inside of me is letting me know that.'"

In John 16:11, Jesus talks about the prince of this world being judged. The Holy Ghost will remind you that you're serving a victorious Lord and you are ruling over a defeated devil. The first time you feel so frustrated and feel like you're going to quit, the Holy Ghost will say, "Wait, the devil's been judged. He doesn't have a right to whip you. Don't give in to him. He's a liar. Stand one more day. Speak it out one more time. Believe God one more minute. Just don't quit because your enemy is defeated and Jesus is Lord. I'm here to convince you that you've got the victory." The devil doesn't stop this stuff just because you got born-again.

If you're not saved, the Holy Spirit is constantly working through ministries, the Word and circumstances to bring Jesus and redemption into your heart, trying to get your attention. The Holy Spirit is constantly working to show you that the devil is defeated; so, don't believe him. The Holy Spirit is telling you, "Jesus has righteousness for you. Come on. You're going to hell if you don't get a change of heart. Come on. I'm going to get you out of this. I'm going to take you up to Jesus." That's what the Holy Spirit's doing. If you're backslid right now, the Holy Spirit is saying, "You can come home tonight. Come on, don't stay back here." If you're sitting right now condemned because you messed up, the Holy Spirit is saying, "It's alright. It's alright. I'll get you through it. Come on. Let's take it up to the altar and lay it down. That's done. Your sins have already been judged in Jesus. All you've got to do is repent of it. Let me help you." When you get born-again, the Holy Spirit comes in. He says, "Let me come into and upon you and give you the power you need to live and be a witness of the Lord Jesus. In John 16:12, Jesus said, "I still have many things to say to you, but you cannot bear them now." (NKJV). There are things in your Christian walk you'll never understand. There are things that God wants to do for you and you'll miss them. You'll go along and people all around you are getting blessed. Somebody is over here praising God, and somebody over here is dancing, and somebody over here is getting blessed, and you're sitting around going, " I don't get it."

You come to church, and we lay hands on the sick. Somebody gets healed or delivered and they fall on the floor and you'll go, "Why is he pushing them down?"

The first time Bonnie ever got a healing, we were in a denominational church and we just prayed and believed. We didn't know anything about the anointing of God. We knew nothing about how to receive healing, we were scripturally illiterate idiots. We knew nothing of the Word. We didn't know anything about the power of God. We just knew God was bigger than they were telling us He was. Bonnie got her healing. We went back to the church Wednesday night and thought we'd give them a good testimony. It was a little denominational church and there were two sections. We were sitting up near the front. Bonnie shared her testimony and said, "The Lord healed me and all the symptoms are gone." I bet eighty percent of the people got up and said, "Can we feel where the knot was on her neck?" They all had to come and see and feel for themselves. She had fingerprints all over her neck where those people came up and touched and said, "It's gone. Ain't it a wonder how that happened?" These people were saved. They were cleansed from sin and had become a vessel of God. The only trouble was they had stopped there. Salvation is first and foremost but God has more for us. We must all be born-again by the work of the Holy Spirit in the new birth. But don't stop there. Now that you're saved let the Lord fill you with the Holy Spirit and empower you to be His witness. Jesus says there are many things that the Lord wants to give you. He wants to show you. He wants to help you with them, but you cannot bear it. You can't understand it. Now look what He says in verse 13, "However, when He, the Spirit of truth, has come, He will guide you into all truth; for He will not speak on His own authority, but whatever He hears He will speak; and He will tell you things to come." (NKJV). There are truths that you'll never have until you get filled with the Holy Ghost. There are things about God you'll not understand or have any comprehension of until you get filled with the Holy Ghost. The Holy Spirit is always eavesdropping on the conversation of the Father and the Son.

He's got an ear to the throne room, and the Father says, "Get ready," and the Lord gets ready. The Holy Ghost says, "You better get ready. He's coming quick. You better get ready." The Lord, the head of the church, says, "Hmm, I believe I'm going to just move in a mighty way. Over the next six months, I'm going to get this people prepared. Then over the next year and a half after that, I'm going to pour out my Spirit like it hasn't ever been poured out and I'm going to heal people. I'm going to send forth that great healing wave across America, or I'm going to send a great move of the miracle signs and wonders." The Holy Ghost says, "Hmm, I better tell folks to get ready. I was hanging out around the throne room, and I heard the Lord say He was getting ready to bring forth a great harvest. He needs some people to get ready. You better get ready. I'm showing you that there's a harvest coming in and there's a move of God coming. You better get ready for it."

Then down inside of you, your spirit starts quickening, and you start getting butterflies in your stomach. You start thinking about it, and you start praying. When you're praying, the Holy Ghost begins to show you that this thing is coming, you begin to get a vision of it, and it becomes real to you. You're all excited about it and you say to someone, "God's getting ready to move." And they say, "What?" You say, "It's just the beginning; God's moving. God's going to move." They look at you like what is wrong here?

You say, "Wait a minute. I thought the whole group here was Christians." They say, "We are." What's the difference? You got a turbo charged home, and they've got an empty one. They've got a pot belly stove in one room warming up to it. You've got a full house of central heat. But you will look around and say, "Don't you get it?" And they don't because there are things that they won't know. It will walk right by them without the Holy Ghost.

He not only shows you things; the Holy Ghost will get you ready for something. He'll say, "Save some money back. I got a deal coming for you." You might be going along and the Spirit of God says, "Listen, I want you to sow this seed right here," and your flesh says, "I can't do it." But your heart says, "I'm going to obey God because the Holy Ghost knows what is coming." He knows if you'll just sow that seed, do this one thing, go witness to that person, go share this good news, go give a hug, or spend a little extra time in prayer what will happen. If you'll just do a few little things, He's maneuvering you in a position to reap the blessing that God has declared as yours.

You can't understand it. Your mind is going crazy with it. Your flesh is screaming, "Why did I do this?" Frustration is trying to set in, but the Holy Ghost is saying, "No, just stick with me. You don't know what's coming, but I've already seen the future. I saw the end from the beginning. I heard it being mentioned. I know what's coming your way." The Holy Ghost will keep you right in there until one day you wake up and you know why you got blessed because you had the power of the Spirit of God operating in your life. He knew how to get you into that place of blessing.

That becomes a witness of the resurrection of Jesus Christ. Some of you husbands and wives, when you get filled with the Holy Ghost, you'll become a better spouse. The Spirit of God will show ladies how to be a good wife. The Spirit of God will show husbands how to take care of your wives. You'll become a better parent. The Spirit of God will show you how to restore broken relationships with your kids. The Spirit of God will show you how to go out here and bring harmony back into the home. The Spirit of God will show you how to get out of debt. The Spirit of God will show you how to walk in victory. The Spirit of God will show you how to get delivered and stay delivered.

You need the Holy Ghost. You need to be filled with the Spirit. Why? You shall receive power, God's divine enabling, and He'll begin to guide you in the truth. He will begin to show you things that are going to come. Jesus goes on to say, "He will glorify Me, for He will take of what is Mine and declare it to you. All things that the Father has are Mine. Therefore I said that He will take of Mine and declare it to you." (John 16:14-15 NKJV). Jesus is saying, "Everything the Father has, He's given it to me now. Because I've done what I was sent to do, my Father has exalted me as Lord, head of the church. He has given to me all power, all glory, all authority, all heaven, all the angels, all everything; everything that the Father has is mine. And when the Holy Spirit comes, He'll take what is mine, which is everything, and show it to you."

Deuteronomy 29:29 says, "The secret things belong to the Lord our God, but those things which are revealed belong to us and to our children forever, that we may do all the words of this law." (NKJV). The Holy Spirit has come to show you that everything God has is available to you, for you, and will work in your life if you'll just learn how to flow.

I want the spirit of revelation operating in my life. I want the Holy Ghost to come and reveal the truth of God to me. I want the Spirit of God. You cannot comprehend in your mind and in your heart the magnitude of how great your God is and what your covenant is with Him until the Spirit of God begins to unveil it to you.

Jesus said, "The Father has given me everything, and the Holy Ghost is going to take everything that I've got and show it to you." Why? So you can walk in it. God is withholding no good thing from them that will walk uprightly before Him. It's a different life. You'll walk a different walk. You'll smile a different smile. You'll shout a different shout. You'll sing a different song. I'm telling you, you'll have a bounce in your step. There'll be an anointing upon your voice that wasn't there before, an anointing in your life that wasn't there before, a wisdom in you and an ability in you that wasn't there before. You were saved before, but now you are equipped. Now you've got the divine enabling of God operating on the inside of you.

You might wonder how you get it. Look in Acts 2 to find out. "When the Day of Pentecost had fully come, they were all with one accord in one place." (v 1 NKJV). First of all, you're going to have to get in one accord with God.

They were right where God told them to be, in accord with what God told them to do. They weren't fighting God anymore. You have got to get to the place where you just surrender. "I surrender myself to the Lord God Almighty. I just give up everything. I turn my life to Jesus."

Acts 2 goes on to say, "And suddenly there came a sound from heaven, as of a rushing mighty wind, and it filled the whole house where they were sitting. Then there appeared to them divided tongues, as of fire, and one sat upon each of them. And they were all filled with the Holy Spirit and began to speak with other tongues, as the Spirit gave them utterance." (vv 2-4 NKJV). To get this, I have to get filled with the Holy Ghost and filled means full. I have got to receive the Holy Ghost into me and upon me until I'm fuller of Him than I am of myself.

The reason we are not doing what God told us to do is we're more full of ourselves than we are of Him. You need to get so full of the Holy Ghost that you surrender to Him and you begin to speak in a heavenly language. If somebody says, "I don't believe in speaking in tongues," then you've aligned yourself with the devil because he doesn't believe in speaking in tongues either. But the apostle Paul believes in speaking in tongues; he told them to not forbid speaking in tongues (see 1 Corinthians 14:39). Apparently, the Lord Jesus believes in it because He told them, "Don't you go anywhere until you get filled." The first thing they did when they got filled was speak in tongues. Do you know why we have such a struggle with speaking in tongues? It's because your spirit should be in rulership of your life. Your spirit should be Lord of your life. God created your spirit to be the king and have dominion over your life. Your mind is the connection between your spirit and the outside world. Your mind should be a servant to your spirit, assisting, and your flesh should be that area of your life where you manifest what the spirit wants to do. The flesh is just where it manifests. It's a slave to the spirit and soul. Flesh has no will of itself. It should only do what it's told to do, but too many of us have made our flesh, our body, the ruler of our life. In so doing, we took our heart into captivity and enthroned our mind, and now our flesh and our mind rules our heart. Therefore, we're more interested in what tickles the flesh instead of what honors God. Your body says, "I would rather do my thing than to do God's thing." What you've got to do is crucify the flesh, bring it back under submission to God, submit to your spirit, get your spirit man filled with the Holy Ghost, and say, "Holy Ghost, take hold together with me and I'm going to speak in tongues and make my flesh surrender to God." What do you need to do to get filled? You just need to come and receive. That's all you do. Just get filled. How do you know when you're filled? You'll talk in tongues.

"How long should I wait? And how long should I struggle?" You shouldn't wait, and you shouldn't have to struggle. You should just go to God and receive and get filled.

Look at Acts 2 again. We're talking about how God moved among those 120 Jewish people. Everybody says, "Well, that was for the Jews." But in Acts 8, we're down to Samaritans, who were half Jews. They weren't full-blooded Jews. The first day, we got the full blood. Now we're in the half blood. "Now when the apostles who were at Jerusalem heard that Samaria had received the word of God, they sent Peter and John to them, who, when they had come down, prayed for them that they might receive the Holy Spirit." (Acts 8:14-15 NKJV). They didn't pray for God to give them the Holy Ghost. They prayed for them to receive the Holy Ghost. These are not full-blooded Jews. They're kind of outskirt Jews. The Jews didn't like them because they didn't come from the same group.

Now we've gone from a hundred percent Jewish people to fifty percent Jewish people. Acts 8 goes on, "For as yet He had fallen upon none of them. They had only been baptized in the name of the Lord Jesus. Then they laid hands on them, and they received the Holy Spirit" (vv 16-17 NKJV). This group got it just like the other group did. So apparently God was no respecter of persons. You didn't have to be one hundred percent Jewish to get it.

Let's go on to Acts 10. Now we've got a group that isn't Jewish at all. This group is just a bunch of Gentiles. This bunch with Cornelius is just hoping that they could get something. Peter's preaching to them: "While Peter was still speaking these words, the Holy Spirit fell upon all those who heard the word. And those of the circumcision who believed were astonished, as many as came with Peter, because the gift of the Holy Spirit had been poured out on the Gentiles also. For they heard them speak with tongues and magnify God" (vv 44-46 NKJV). "They of the circumcision," those that were one hundred percent Jewish, were saying, "We can't believe this. Look what's going on here with this bunch of Gentiles. This bunch of Gentiles with no claim at all to our covenant blessings—I can't believe this. If God would give it to them, He will give it to anybody who will believe."

I want you to know that it doesn't matter what your genealogy is. It doesn't matter what your pedigree or your family tree is. If you just walked in off the street and turned your life to Jesus Christ, you can get filled with the Holy Ghost, just like somebody whose grandparents preach and their daddy's a priest. It doesn't matter what kind of bloodline you come from. What matters is if Jesus is your Lord. You don't have to have an ancestral tree of great prophets to be used of God.

That's why you come and get filled with the Holy Ghost because God takes nobodies and turns them into somebodies and divinely enables them to become great warriors in the kingdom of God.

You need to be filled with the Holy Ghost. If you're dry, you need to be filled with the Holy Ghost. If you've lost your joy, you need to be filled with the Holy Ghost. If you're struggling in your walk with

God, you need to be filled with the Holy Ghost. If you can't praise God, you need to be filled with the Holy Ghost. You need to be full of God. You need to have that. If you've struggled with your flesh, you need to be filled with the Holy Ghost. If you've come through a traumatic experience recently, you need to be filled with the Holy Ghost. Ephesians 5:18 says you need to be filled. You need to stay filled.

There's one initial baptism in the Holy Ghost. When you get the fullness of it, you'll speak in tongues, and you won't apologize for speaking in tongues. Whenever you speak in tongues, you'll look back and you'll say, "Come on, gang. It's fun." That old gang may be saying, "I don't believe in speaking in tongues," but as you continue walking in the this new and greater walk with the Lord, they will want what you have.

But once you've been filled with the Holy Ghost, you need to stay full of the Holy Ghost. When it's a difficult time in your life, don't get caught up so much in the battle that you don't spend time in the tent with the commander in chief. The harder the battle you're going through, the more you need to pray in tongues and worship God and spend time with God. I've been guilty of this, and God convicted my heart. Too many times, we find ourselves in a real hard struggle, in a battle. We find ourselves fighting skirmishes, fighting this, and trying to take care of it. We've got our armor on, but we didn't take time to get with the commander in chief, the Lord Jesus, and spend time in the Spirit and let the Holy Ghost empower us. Remember, you'll receive power after the Holy Ghost comes upon you. Your power doesn't come by wielding the sword. The power comes by being full of God.

If you're in the midst of a great battle right now, or if you're going through some struggles, don't let the devil say, "You don't have time to worship. You don't have time to minister." Go make time: make time for an hour of praying in the Spirit and fellowshipping with the Lord in the Spirit in the throne room of God. That will accomplish more for you than two hours of battling out here in the flesh. It'll keep you refreshed. Jude 20 says, "But you, beloved, building yourselves up on your most holy faith, praying in the Holy Spirit" (NKJV).

The only requirement to receive the baptism of the Holy Spirit, to speak in tongues and be endued with power is to be born-again. Once we have made Jesus Lord of our life and are born of the Spirit, we can now receive the fullness of the Holy Spirit or as Acts 2:38 says, "the gift of the Holy Spirit" (NKJV).

If you have not yet received the Gift of the Holy Spirit, I encourage you to pray this prayer and be filled with the Holy Spirit.

Dear Heavenly Father,

I thank you for bringing me into the family of God. I believe in my heart and confess with my mouth that Jesus Christ, Your Son, is my Lord and Savior. I am a Child of God, a new creation in Christ Jesus. You said in Luke 11:13, "If you then, being evil, know how to give good gifts to your children, how much more will your heavenly Father give the Holy Spirit to those who ask Him!" (NKJV). You are my Father and I am Your Child and I am asking You now to give me the Holy Spirit in His fullness. Thank You for granting my request and right now I believe I receive the Holy Spirit coming in me and upon me, giving me the power to be Your witness. I also receive my spiritual prayer language so I can pray in tongues as the Spirit gives me utterance. So, by faith, I receive the baptism of the Holy Spirit and by faith, I begin to speak in tongues. Thank You Heavenly Father, I believe I am now filled with the Spirit. In Jesus' Name, Amen.

CPSIA information can be obtained
at www.ICGtesting.com
Printed in the USA
BVHW051227300623
666567BV00009B/14